RUSLAN &
LUDMILA

RUSLAN
LUDMILA

ALEXANDER
PUSHKIN

translated by D. M. Thomas

RUSLAN & LUDMILA

ALEXANDER PUSHKIN

translated by D. M. Thomas

SCRIBNER

LONDON NEW YORK TORONTO SYDNEY NEW DELHI

First published in Russian in 1820

This English edition published in Great Britain by Scribner,
an imprint of Simon & Schuster UK Ltd, 2019
A CBS COMPANY

English language translation Copyright © D. M. Thomas, 2019

SCRIBNER and design are registered trademarks of The Gale Group, Inc.,
used under licence by Simon & Schuster Inc.

The right of D. H. Thomas to be identified as author of this work has been asserted
in accordance with the Copyright, Designs and Patents Act, 1988.

1 3 5 7 9 10 8 6 4 2

Simon & Schuster UK Ltd
1st Floor
222 Gray's Inn Road
London WC1X 8HB

Simon & Schuster Australia, Sydney
Simon & Schuster India, New Delhi

www.simonandschuster.co.uk
www.simonandschuster.com.au
www.simonandschuster.co.in

A CIP catalogue record for this book
is available from the British Library

Hardback ISBN: 978-1-4711-7745-3
eBook ISBN: 978-1-4711-7746-0

Typeset by M Rules
Printed and bound by CPI Group (UK) Ltd, Croydon, CR0 4YY

Preface

About the work

The year 2020 is the bicentenary of what may be regarded as the beginning of Russian literature, with its noble history of defending freedom and spiritual values.

For it was in 1820 that *Ruslan and Ludmila* was published, the first major work by Alexander Pushkin, the greatest Russian poet (part-African by ancestry) and the founder of Russia's literature and indeed of its modern language. He was just twenty years old, and had begun the poem in 1817 when he was still at school. Based on his country's folklore, transformed into art, it created an instant sensation: acclaim on one side, wrath on the other. In the words of John Bayley: '*Ruslan* contains in embryo all the genius of Pushkin's later poems.'

About the translator

D. M. Thomas is a British poet and novelist. His novel *The White Hotel* (1981) became a worldwide bestseller, published in thirty languages. He has also been acclaimed for his translations of Anna Akhmatova and Pushkin (*The Bronze Horseman and Other Poems* (Penguin, 1982) and *Onegin* (Francis Boutle, 2011)). Of the former, Erica Jong wrote, 'D. M. Thomas makes this astounding poet available to us as if for the first time.' His biography *Alexander Solzhenitsyn: A Century in His Life* won the Orwell Prize. He lives in Cornwall, his birthplace, with his fourth wife.

TRANSLATOR'S INTRODUCTION

In the summer of 2017 I was suffering a distress familiar to authors – and perhaps especially elderly authors: writer's block. After a few weeks of staring all day at a blank screen, I decided enough was enough and I would indulge myself by seeking the company of an old friend, Pushkin. More than any other poet I know he invites friendship, often interjecting a greeting into his poetry: 'My friends ...' or 'My dear friends ...' I know that he is mostly addressing the fellow pupils he met at the Imperial Lyceum at Tsarskoe Selo, friendships which became lifelong; but his openness, his geniality, his sense of fun, seem to invite and welcome even a British poet attempting to translate his work two centuries later. He greatly respected, and often relied on, translations, which he described as 'the post-horses of enlightenment'.

I have spent some of the happiest periods of my life with him beside me in my study. The last such period was in 2010, when for many months I lived and breathed his great verse novel *Onegin*. It was high time we met again. But which work would it be? I had translated so much of him. There was one famous work I had always neglected, skated over, dismissing it as juvenilia: *Ruslan and Ludmila*. I did not even know its plot, except vaguely that it was about witches and sorcerers. All right, *Ruslan* it would be. It was long; it would engage me for months.

I made a resolution, which I have kept to, that I would read up nothing about it until I had finished. It has meant that every incident, every line, was a surprise. I was in the position of its first readers, who received it with an excitement never before known in Russia over a literary work. The work of a twenty-year-old youth! Not quite a great poem but a very fine and dazzling one: so much so that the most famous poet of his age, Zhukovsky, sent him a self-portrait with the noble inscription, 'From a pupil to his master'.

I experienced a similar excitement and exhilaration – alongside the impossible but joyful work of trying to convey a little of his maturing mastery of his chosen verse form, the tetrameter. As John Bayley observed: 'The reader is conscious of no stricture in the verse medium, but only of its powers of liberation'. The English Muse is much more at home with the pentameter.

What is less hard to convey is his brilliance at shaping the narrative. He has constructed it out of the 'magic' tales he heard from the lips of his beloved childhood nurse, and from his reading. His poem moves about among the adventures of four knights, including Ruslan, separately seeking Ludmila, abducted on her wedding night, and her plight in captivity. The brio of the ever-changing narrative never lets up. Pushkin draws us into this world of sorcery and witchcraft, making us believe in it – even while he often playfully satirises it. The sorcery he describes seems almost a metaphor for his own creative sorcery.

He can switch the mood from dark to light to dark again in an instant. At one point in his quest for his stolen bride Ruslan comes across a huge mound, which turns out to be a living head, planted on the plain by a treacherous magus, his brother. Ruslan comes up close and finds the head is asleep. He tickles its nostrils with his lance to wake it; the head sneezes, releasing a whole colony of owls. (This enraged conservative reviewers, who believed poetry should be beautiful and heroic always.) It is grotesquely funny; yet when Ruslan next confronts the head during his ride home the mood changes to one of painful and moving tragedy.

Only Pushkin among poets can achieve this, I think; though one is reminded of the mixture of sadness and humour in Chekhov's plays. Indeed the first two lines of Pushkin's famous Prologue (added in 1828) are quoted three times in *Three Sisters*. Just as all of Pushkin's later poetry exists in embryo in *Ruslan*, all of Russian literature is in embryo in Pushkin's works.

When I had completed the translation, with the customary mixture of satisfaction and sadness, only then did I research the poem. And found the pleasing coincidence that I had written my version precisely two hundred years after Pushkin, aged eighteen, had begun to write *Ruslan* at his school. Once he had left the Lyceum, he wrote between spells of dissipation and illness (often connected). I love this account of one convalescence by his biographer Henri Troyat:

Friends who came to call found him stretched on a bed in a striped dressing gown with a skullcap on his head. Everything – tables, clothes, floor – was littered with papers and books . . . But the moment he was on his feet again, he abandoned it and resumed his wild career, reappearing, with the face of one risen from the dead, in drawing room and theatre, gambling house, dive and bordello.

He continued to wear the skullcap, and I suspect it reappears, with magic powers, in *Ruslan*.

He eventually grew somewhat bored with the poem, which concludes with a slightly discordant 'heroic' battle scene, Rus' against the Pechenegs. By the time *Ruslan* appeared in print in St Petersburg, he had offended the Tsar by writing subversive political poems and been banished to the Caucasus. In a moving Epilogue, written there, he laments (rather prematurely!) that his poetic Muse has gone, and with her the 'blissful, silent days' of creation. 'Peace and freedom' were what he always longed for, tranquil, solitary times in which, for all his seeming fluency, he polished and repolished every line. I suspect he welcomed the illnesses which would lead to convalescence and the reappearance of the Muse, smiling down at the dishevelled poet in his magic skullcap.

He had already lived more than half his life. In the

next seventeen years he would write masterpieces in every genre.

When he was carried home to die in his study, following his duel in 1837, his doctor asked: 'Do you not want to say goodbye to your friends?' Pushkin waved his arm weakly around the book-lined room and said, 'Farewell, my friends!'

Farewell again, my friend!

DMT
Truro, Cornwall, 2017
www.dmthomasonline.net

Dedication

Girls at whose touch my spirit trembled,
For you, my loves, each one a queen,
For you alone I have assembled
In hours of idleness, serene,
These fables whispered down the ages;
The hand recording them is true:
Accept, I pray, my playful pages;
I've no desire for praise from you,
Content if some love-troubled lady,
In woods with scarcely light to see,
Will scan these verses, far too shady
To show the world she's reading me.

Prologue

A green oak by the salt sea weathered;
And to it by a gold chain bound
A highly learned cat is tethered,
Who on the chain goes round and round:
Walks to the left – he tells a story,
Walks to the right – a song he sings.

What wonders there! There, goblins scurry;
A mermaid to an oak branch clings;
On paths lost where the forest thickens
Are tracks of beasts not seen before;
A hut stands on the feet of chickens,

Without a window or a door;
Visions fill wood and vale; there, idle
Soft-plashing waves at sunrise sidle
Over the barren beach's sand,
And thirty armoured knights a-glitter
Advance out of the clear, bright water,
A grizzled Sea-king in command;
There, I shall mention just in passing,
A prince holds captive a fierce Tsar;
There, people watch, through dark clouds massing,
A warlock who's just come in sight,
High up, and carrying a knight,
All wonder if they've travelled far.
A princess, locked up, grieves most cruelly,
Although a brown wolf serves her truly;
There, Baba Yaga, in a mortar,
Sweeps herself over wood and water;
There Tsar Kashchei drools on his gold;
All breathes of Rus' ... the Rus' of old!
There too was I, much sweet mead drinking
As under the green oak I sat,
Listening to tales I marvelled at
Spun by the circling cat, deep-thinking.
One of his stories I recall,
And I will share it with you all ...

CANTO ONE

I bring to light a vanished day,
Deeds that survived the ages' testing.

Vladimir the Bright-Sun held sway
In a high banquet chamber, feasting
With doughty sons and friends. The host
Rose smiling to propose a toast,
Raising head-high his heavy glass,
To Prince Ruslan, to whom will pass
His youngest daughter. As with most
Feasts in old Russia, all was measured,
Quite slow; such was the ceremony

RUSLAN AND LUDMILA

Of feasts, the eating, drinking, leisured;
The goblets circled without hurry,
The bearers moved about quite gravely,
Keeping the company well-wined,
With lots of froth; as was behovely,
Then steeply, from the waist, inclined.

Talk, laughs, created an unceasing
And joyous buzz the table round;
Then, over all, a voice most pleasing
And, too, a lyre's sweet rippling sound;
Now all were silent, and delighted
To hear the enchanting bard Bayan
Singing of Lel* who has united
Lovely Ludmila and Ruslan.

Into impatient longing sinking,
Ruslan is scarcely eating, drinking;
Darling Ludmila holds his gaze,
He burns, he knits his brows, he sighs,
Absently plucks at his moustache and

* Slavic god of love

Counts every second, deep-impassioned.
Elsewhere amidst the noisy crowd,
Gloomily hunched and beetle-browed,
Sitting aloof, are three knights, youthful,
Staring into their empty cups,
Of the rich meats don't eat a mouthful;
For them the mead-jug never stops;
They do not hear the wise Bayan;
These guests, three rivals of Ruslan,
Along with love have the dread poison
Of hate, incapable of reason.
First, brave Rogdai, who with his blade
Flashing in many battles made
Wider rich Kiev's fertile fields;
Next, loudmouthed Farlaf, never bested
At feasts, but when in battle tested
He becomes humble and soon yields;
His passions tautened like a drum –
The third, the Khazar Khan Ratmir.
All three sit pale and sunk in gloom,
The cheerful feast brings them no cheer.

Now it was done. Clatter and jangled
Voices as everyone rose and mingled,

All eyes now on the bridal pair:
The bride with downcast eyes, demure, or
As if her heart felt sudden terror,
The groom now with a joyous air.
Over the earth night's shadows creeping,
The murk of midnight moving close,
The boyars make their bows; half-sleeping
From the strong mead, they take to horse.
The groom, in rapture, with elation,
Is stroking in imagination
The bashful maiden in their bed;
Her father, sad in secret, tender,
Draws in the air the sign to render
His blessing on these newly wed.

The bride's escorted by her servants
To the silk couch; the torches dim;
But Lel, in customary observance,
Is ready ... The night-lamp's lit by him.
The wedding gifts at last unfurl,
Fondest desires are coming true;
Falls jealous raiment from the girl
On carpets of the richest hue ...
Do you not hear the whispers, amorous,

The liquid, sweet sound of a kiss,
Her interrupted, troubled murmur as
The final shyness yields? ... No, *this*
You hear – the sudden, monstrous
    crashing
Of thunder ... shattered, their delight –
The room's lit by the lightning flashing,
Then darkness; quenched is the nightlight,
Smoke pours in and the dark room sways
And trembles; Ruslan is in a daze,
Feeling his brave heart turn to ice
And he lies helpless; now, an eerie
Voice sounds in the nuptial chamber,
    twice,
Someone still blacker than the dreary
Room looms up ... and then in a trice
Vanishes ... Now all noise is stilled;
Starts up the bridegroom, terror-filled,
The sweat upon his brow is frozen;
Shaking, he searches with cold hand
The dark he cannot understand ...
O grief! his love, his bride, his chosen ...
He might be plucking at the wind,
For his Ludmila is not there,
Borne away by some unknown power.

*

If you love hopelessly and madly,
Endure all torments love can give,
My friends, you will live bleakly, sadly,
Yet it is possible to live.
But if, after the long, long years,
At last you are in bed embracing
The object of your longings, tears,
Just for a moment your heart racing,
But then your love is snatched away ...
My friends, I know I'd rather die!

Ruslan was still alive, tormented.
What of the great Prince? Soon informed,
He summoned all his court, demented –
His friends, his sons, Ruslan, and stormed
At him, his grief and anger blazing:
'Where is my daughter – and your bride?'
His son-in-law, his gaze not raising,
Seemed not to hear. Vladimir cried:
'My knights, my friends, beyond all praising
Your service; now pity an old man!
Who'll save my precious girl, my life?

10

Of gratitude you will find no lack. –
Weep, wretch! You could not guard your wife! –
Whoever finds and brings her back,
In honour of his manly courage
Shall have my daughter's hand in marriage
And half my realm.' Ruslan cried, 'I!'
'I! I!' then shouted out Rogdai,
A plea that with Farlaf's shout mingled;
'We'll straight to horse!' came Ratmir's cry;
With secret joy his body tingled;
'We'll search the earth – if need be, sky!'
Mutely the old man's mouth beseeches.
– 'Our lord, our master, no more speeches,
Fear not, we'll bring back the princess.'
In tears Vladimir's gnarled hand stretches
To bid farewell to them and bless.

All four together leave the palace.
Ruslan is ashen, colour quelled
And life quenched by the unearthly malice
That stole the bride he'd barely held.
Their steeds are off as soon as mounted,
And soon a dozen versts they've counted
The Dnieper's fruitful banks along,

11

A cloud of dust behind them flung;
They've long since vanished, yet Vladimir
Stands gazing after, and believes
He can still see them, as a dreamer
Still sees dead friends for whom he grieves.

Ruslan rode silent, like a spectre,
His mind and memory in a trance.
Behind him, in his mind a Hector,
Farlaf was full of arrogance;
Hands on his hips he rode, reliant
On his brave steed, crying, 'My friends,
Freedom at last! The waiting ends!
When do you think we'll meet the giant?
I see him fall, his hot blood poured,
That blood with passions so repulsive!
Rejoice, rejoice, my trusty sword,
Rejoice, my steed, so eager, restive!'

The Khazar Khan is in his dreams
Already the princess embracing:
He's dancing on his horse, it seems,
So madly his young blood is racing;

The flame of hope is in his eyes,
He drives his steed until it flies,
Then, teasing, makes him stand and frolic,
Turn a tight circle and then rear,
Then scale a hill that's almost sheer.

Rogdai is wrathful, full of colic,
Silent, fearing a fate unknown,
On helpless jealousy he's gnawing
Angrily, as a dog a bone;
Like wolves, atrocious thoughts are clawing
At him; his eyes seek out Ruslan.

The shades of night were growing deeper;
All day they'd travelled the one road,
These rivals, following the Dnieper.
Soon nothing of the river showed,
And the tired horses needed resting . . .
Sleep held all; Dnieper cold and black.
But with the first bright sunlight cresting
A mountain's flank they saw the track
Split into four. 'Time we divided,
Embraced our destiny, win or lose.'

They mounted, and their steeds, unguided,
Headed whichever way each chose.

What do you do, enwrapped in sadness,
Ruslan, alone in endless steppes?
Ludmila, and that night of madness,
Was all of it a dream perhaps?
Over your brows your bronze helm sunken,
Slowly you feel your spirit shrunken,
Riding through the deserted lands,
The reins loose in your weakened hands.
Hope dies, and faith is barely gleaming.

A cave appears, cuts short his dreaming;
A light within. Straightway he stands
Inside. Through caverns brooding, twisted,
Carved out when nature first existed,
He walks, despondent. But what's this?
An old man with a bright, clear face,
A grey beard; near, a lamp is burning,
And with a peaceful, benign look
He's reading from an ancient book,
Intent; slowly the leaves he's turning.

'I bid you welcome here, my son!' –
The old man greeted, with a smile.
– 'These twenty years I've lived alone
In gloom here, withering the while.
But now at last has come the day
I've long expected, long awaited;
Our meeting in this way was fated;
Sit down and hear me out, I pray.
Your spirit's low without Ludmila,
Knowing you let somebody steal her
Away; but evil cannot last:
Take heart, and seize the moment, fast.
Say to your fainting thoughts, begone!
All that is lost can be recovered;
With faith and hope – and sword –
     fare forward,
Make haste towards the midnight sun!

Ruslan, the wretched malefactor
Is the dread wizard Chernomor,
Of lovely girls a known abductor;
He's taken your princess, I'm sure.
He saw her, luscious fruit, and plucked her.
No one has broken through the door

To the retreat where he is doctor
Of the black arts, high on a hill;
But you can, if you have the will.
Enough! I'm tired; speech is a labour
After long silence. Go and kill
Your bride's abductor with your sabre.'

Our knight fell at the old man's feet
And planted on his hand a kiss,
The world with joy again replete,
For heart's ache, once relieved, seems bliss.
His face, so gloomy earlier, lightened
– But then it darkened once again.
'I know the reason for your pain;
Though sorrow's noose is quickly tightened,' –
The old man said; – 'My son, you're frightened
Of what his lechery may bring;
Fear not: he feels old age's blight, and
With a young girl can't do a thing.
Oh, when he whistles the moon faints,
He makes the stars run off and cower
Beneath the horizon; but against
The laws of time he has no power.
He is her warder, madly jealous,

Her cell he'll lock, the key will hide,
Is her tormentor, ruthless, zealous,
But she remains – your spotless bride.
He walks around her, silent, fuming,
Cursing the burden in his breast . . .
But now the day outside is glooming,
Ruslan; it's time for you to rest.'

On soft moss Prince Ruslan is lying
Before a fire that's almost done.
He tries to find oblivion
In sleep, but turns and tosses, sighing . . .
To the old man he speaks at last:
'Father, my day-thoughts hold me fast,
I sleep unsleeping; desolation
Is all I see, my soul feels faint.
I badly need, mysterious saint,
Your spiritual conversation.
You are a soul the Fates confide in,
And you've been kind to me. Would you
Confide to me who sent you to
This wilderness all life has died in?'

*

Sighing, and with a smile forlorn,
He spoke: 'I have forgotten, child,
My old existence in a wild,
Bleak land. In Finland was I born,
A land of humble folk and labours.
Shepherd-boy to my village neighbours,
In hidden valleys only known
To us, I kept the flocks, carefree,
Loved streams and woods, and being alone:
Such the small pleasures poverty
Allows. But not for long was given
To me that comfortable haven.

Into my peaceful life – confusion.
Like a flower blooming in seclusion
Naïna lived. All girls were shadows,
Lovely enough, where I abode.
One morning with my flock I strode,
Piping, across some dusky meadows,
And saw, beside a rippling brook,
Weaving a garland, concentrating,
Naïna. There my fate was waiting.
I stopped attending to my flock.
She looked the same – yet not the same:

No village maid – a regal look.
The flame of love was my reward there
For staring at her with no shame;
I was becalmed in her, was moored there . . .
First love, that will not come again;
I felt its bliss, I felt its pain.

It took six months from when I'd seen her
Transformed for me to dare to say,
Trembling, *I love you*, to Naïna.
How I remember that dark day!
She showed complete indifference,
Tossing her hair, as if she knew
Her beauty might entice a prince:
Well, shepherd boy. I don't love you!
My sheep became like snarling leopards;
The shady groves, our homely food,
The happy games with fellow shepherds –
I saw but darkness, nothing good,
My heart as dry as half-burnt wood.
And finally I fixed my mind
To leave our Finnish fields behind,
Take to the sea as my arena,
Win fame with men of martial blood

Beside me: surely then I could
Soften the heart of proud Naïna.
I called on lusty fishermen
To fish for gold by facing dangers;
My fatherland was peaceful then,
Leaving the clash of swords to strangers,
But now they heard the havoc when
Canoes and blades clashed. Far I travelled
With fearless fellow countrymen,
In blizzards, stormy waves, we revelled,
Ferociously we fought for ten
Bloodthirsty years. Our fame took flight and
Princes abroad became dismayed
As their defenders vanished, frightened
By the mere rumour of a raid.
We laughed amid the clamorous broils,
A merry band, and never ceased
To be good comrades; shared the spoils,
And with defeated foes we'd feast.
But in my heart was still Naïna;
Amid the noise of feast or war
A secret sorrow, ever keener,
Drew me towards our Finnish shore.
It's time for home! Time to set sail,
My friends, I said, and hang our mail

Under our eaves! Soon oars were creaking,
We left behind the fearsome trail
And dreamt of landing, rich and hale
And proud – each one of us a Sea-king!

I had achieved all I had wanted,
My ten years' dream; I was on fire,
By her at last, at last, confronted:
Ah, life held nothing lovelier!
I laid before her feet, enraptured,
My sword that so much blood had captured
It smelt of it ... Gold, coral, pearls ...
Around her, silent, envious girls,
Her pals. I said, *I love you*. She,
Her eyes upon some distant view,
Addressed her slave disdainfully:
Well, hero, but I don't love you!

But why relate to you, my son,
Events I find beyond endurance?
Akh, even now, alone, alone,
Awaiting only death's appearance,
My soul already numb, before

My eyes right now, and in my hearing,
Are her cold look and words. Tears pour
Down my old cheeks, you see –
      still searing.
But hear: along our northern shore
Were fishermen who knew the lore
Of magic; spells they cast while steering.
Eternal silence all around,
At sea, or amid endless birches,
Greybearded wizards could be found,
In magic science their researches,
Leading to wisdom most profound.
Madness, for any to insult them,
They knew the past, the future, of
One's life; and fearful to consult them:
They could cast spells for death – or love.

I therefore, grieving and despairing,
For love of her all dangers daring,
Began to think that sorcery might
Work on Naïna, proud, uncaring,
And a responsive love ignite.
Seeking the teaching of the sages,
I passed much time in wandering through

The deepest forests, I withdrew
To learn the wisdom of the ages.
There came the moment long since
  sought,
I could decipher nature's pages,
Saw all with clarity of thought.
I learned the power of incantation,
And revelled in that revelation!
Now, now, Naïna, thou art mine,
The crown of love is mine and thine!
Victory is ours, though late.
The victor though, in truth, was fate.

So dense the forest no light gleams
Where I, aglow with youthful dreams,
With rapturous hope and expectation,
Summon up with an invocation
The spirits ... straightway thunder rumbles,
The trees bend to a whirlwind's roar,
The earth beneath me cracks and crumbles ...
And then I see, sitting before
Me, an old woman, her back a hoop,
Head shaky, grey and sparse her hair,
Her eyes are sunken, her dugs droop:

Senility in form, demeanour ...
Akh, my dear knight, that was Naïna! ...
I could not speak, numb, horrified,
Gazed long upon this apparition
So dire, and doubted my own vision;
Tears welling in my eyes, I cried:
"Is it possible? Can this be truly
You, my Naïna? Ah, my love,
Your beauty, where ...? The gods above,
Can they have altered you so cruelly?
Tell me, it can't be long since I
Left light and life to live among
The shamans in these woods? Not long? ..."
– "Some forty years," was her reply,
"Seventy I became this morning!"
– Her voice a croak. "But it's no matter,
The years fly by, like leaves they scatter,
Our springs have vanished without
          warning,
To reach old age we have succeeded!
The joys of youth are unreliable;
I may not have the charms I had,
I've lost some teeth, as gums receded,
Flesh is less firm, and limbs less pliable,
I'm possibly hunchbacked, a tad.

But really, friend, it's not so bad,
I have my virtues nonetheless:
You see, I am a sorceress!"

And Ruslan, what she said was true.
I stood dumb, shaken to the core;
I was a fool, for all I knew
Of the dark arts, of secret lore.

But what was dreadful, I'd applied all
The right spells, but had come to grief
In spite of it. My shrivelled idol
Burned with a lust beyond belief.
Her ghastly mouth, sucked inwards, broke
Into a ghastlier smile, a croak
Confessed her love, and rapture offered.
You can imagine how I suffered!
I trembled, I cast down my eyes;
She whined out, through a fit of coughing,
Her proposition in this wise:
"I know now that my heart is loving,
For tender passion was it born;
Dear love, my coldness I now mourn,

My feelings slept too long, I'm burning;
I'll die unless we two are pressed
As one together, breast to breast . . .
My dearest darling, feel me yearning! . . ."

Not only that – she gazed, Ruslan,
Gazed with her old eyes, languid, humbled;
Not only that – at my kaftan
With her thin, bony hands she fumbled;
Not only that – I felt faint, gasping,
From terror of her beady stare;
I knew it was too much to bear,
I screamed and ran, lungs gulping, rasping.
She after me: "O soul infernal!
You have disturbed my peace eternal,
The bright, clear days of a pure maid!
You could not see my heart's still vernal!
Despised me – but that's men all over!
We're wooed at first, but then betrayed!
It took me too long to discover
That truth; you lied right from the start,
And lured me to betray my heart . . .
Seducer! Monster! Evil shaman!
But fear, you pirate, a robbed woman!"

*

We parted then with that ill omen.
Since then I've lived in isolation,
With worldly values disenchanted,
And with an old man's consolation,
Study, and the sweet peace it's granted.
I fade just like these fading embers;
But all the feelings she once felt
The ancient woman still remembers:
The love which made her coldness melt
Has turned to all her life's Decembers.
With only black thoughts to sustain her
And give her energy, Naïna
Will hate you too, since you are male;
But evil, in the end, must fail.'

Unheard, the quiet flight of night
As Ruslan attentively had listened
To the long tale of love and fate.
When from outside the dawn rays glistened
Our knight felt charged, his eyes were bright
Though he had scarcely drowsed. Embracing
The old man, and warm thanks expressing,

He left the cave. The sky was blue,
And Ruslan felt hope surging through
His soul. He'd had enough of rest,
And whistled as his steed he leapt on.
'Be with me, father, in my quest!'
The bold horse pawed the ground it stepped on,
Then they were off. 'My son, Godspeed!'
The old man cried. 'Live a good life!
Forgive and bless and love your wife,
And of this old man's words take heed!'

Canto Two

Will you, his rivals in this mission,
Find peace among yourselves at least,
Or turn to strife, swords in collision,
Gorging on violence's feast? . . .

Courageous Rogdai, in a mood
Of half-submerged disquietude,
Left at the crossways his companions
And journeyed through a solitude
Comprising tangled woods and canyons;
With him, an unseen icy chill,
An evil spirit rode, dismaying

Further his muted heart and will.
He tried to cheer himself by saying,
'Beware, the lot of you! I'll kill! ...
Ruslan! You above all take heed:
You will not see your bride's tears spilt ...'
And suddenly he turns his steed
Around, and rides back at full tilt.

The ever fearless knight Farlaf
Had spent all morning in a dream,
Woke when the sun had circled half,
Then set to eat, beside a stream,
To work his moral torpor off,
A pheasant pie in a sour cream.
Then he sees someone on the plain,
Distant, but heading straight for him,
And riding like a hurricane.
A knight at arms, no friendly farmer.
Farlaf leaves pie, spear, helmet, armour,
Leaps on his horse and is away,
Not looking back. 'You coward, stay!'
He hears the shout. 'And if you don't
My sword will hack you till it's blunt!'
Farlaf in full flight almost fainted

On recognising Rogdai's voice,
A knight with murder well acquainted;
Death or escape his only choice,
He speeds the more. So will a hare
Prick back his ears from sudden fear,
Leap across fields and woods and mounds
In terror of the chasing hounds.
Spring had the winter's snowfall melted
And churned the earth into a slush
Where Farlaf and his bold steed pelted,
And in the springtime torrents' rush
A wide ditch had been gouged.
　　　The horse,
Swishing its tail, its white mane shaking,
Took the steel bit, and without breaking
Its stride it gamely leapt across.
Its rider goes head over heels
And pitches in the filthy ditch,
And lies, not knowing which is which,
Earth, heaven, everything so reels.
Prepares for death, for here's Rogdai
Leaning above, his sword drawn. 'Die,
Poltroon!' Then Farlaf, scarcely breathing,
He recognises, and chagrin,
Surprise and anger can be seen

In Rogdai's face; his sword he's sheathing
Reluctantly. Emits an oath,
Rides swiftly off. And not long after,
There comes from him a gentle laughter;
At Farlaf or himself? Why, both.

Soon after, on an upward trail,
He met a crone, thin as a matchstick,
Barely alive, humpbacked and frail.
She feebly lifted up her crutch-stick;
'That's where you'll find him,' she predicted,
Pointing the stick towards the north;
Buoyed by this help, so unexpected,
He gaily rode towards his death.

But what of Farlaf? In the ditch
He lay, not breathing; mud his bedding.
'I'm either dead or dying. Which?
Where is my wicked rival heading? ...'
Then of a sudden, from above,
He heard the crone's voice, deep and gruff:
'Get up, young man, all's calm around you;
You're fortunate that I have found you.

I've brought your horse, and once you've risen
And pulled yourself together, listen . . .'

On all fours the embarrassed knight
Crawled slowly out and stood upright,
Gazed at the crone and all around,
Sighed with relief, no foes in sight,
And said, 'Thank God, I'm safe and sound!'

'Believe me,' said the kind old lady,
'By you Ludmila won't be found;
You have had trials enough already;
Far away she has gone to ground.
Roaming the world's not worth a rouble;
Don't you agree, you've done your best, dear?
Take my advice: stay out of trouble,
Don't rub a sore to make it fester.
Go home to your Kiev estate
And live there quietly without fuss;
The joys of solitude are great;
Ludmila you can leave to us.'

*

She disappeared. Accepting fate,
The knight decided not to roam
But sensibly to ride back home.
Completely lost his lust for glory
And even wanting the princess.
A sound behind him made him hurry;
Even the flight of a tomtit,
Or a stream's murmur, made him sweat.

Meanwhile Prince Ruslan is far distant,
Through fields and forests riding blind;
The same tormenting and insistent
Questions keep racing through
          his mind . . .
'Ludmila, shall we meet again?
Where are you? Are you dead? In pain?
I'll see your sweet face once more, surely,
And hear your voice that rings so purely?
Or will you always be imprisoned
By the old wizard, lose your bloom,
Becoming, as the years pass, wizened,
In a dark dungeon, like a tomb?
Or will my rivals, sunk in vice,
Seize you? No, pearl beyond price,

No! No! While I still have my head
And sword, and wicked blood to shed!'

Once, when the day had turned to
        gloaming,
Upon a winding path and steep
He rode; below, a river roaming;
Everything quiet as a sleep.
A humming arrow past him flies;
The clank of armour, whinnies, cries,
Came from behind him on the path,
Its peace transformed to sounds of wrath.
'Stay where you are!' a voice came growling.
He looked behind, along the dim
Track, turned his steed about, then,
        scowling,
Rode calmly back to deal with him.
'Aha! Ruslan! At last I've found you!
Look at the wilderness around you
For this is where you will have died,
In bed with worms and not your bride.'
That growling voice he knew too well . . .

*

My friends! you're wondering what befell
That girl he longs to sleep beside!
I've been too long a kind of gaoler,
I should unlock the heavy door
So you can see and hear Ludmila
And the atrocious Chernomor.

Confidants of my impolite
Fantasies, I told the story
Of how, in an indecent foray,
Ludmila, in the dark of night,
Was from Ruslan, inflamed by passion,
Torn away in unseemly fashion.
Unhappy maiden! when that rogue,
Your blissful union to prorogue,
Transformed your peaceful joy to panic,
He bore you upwards to a cloud,
Unseen through fog and smoke satanic,
Then in a trice to his abode
High on a mountaintop. You swooned;
In the dread castle of the wizard,
Like a poor beggar in a blizzard
Her flesh like ice, you were marooned.

*

So have I seen, in my own yard,
Hot summer summoning up the blood,
The sultan of the henhouse chasing
A nervous hen, cluck-clucking, racing
To get away; but there's no stopping
The impassioned rooster, and the hen
Submits to powerful wings ... But then
A circling, watchful kite comes dropping
Out of the heavens, lightning-swift:
Seizes, flies up, a lightning lift,
The poor hen helpless in his talons,
Past fearful crags to his dark eyrie
Unreachable by humans, where he
– Does a kite's work. The rest is silence.
The rooster can but call and mourn
For his lost love, and watch her airy
Feathers and fluff come floating down.

Till morning the unwilling guest
Unstirring lay, as if in death,
Though dreadful visions passed beneath
Her calm eyelids. And when these passed,

RUSLAN AND LUDMILA

On waking up, she was possessed
Both by desire and agitation:
Still felt the wedding night's elation
And longed for ... something more ... at last.
Whispers: 'My dearest, come, O come!' ...
But then with fear was stricken dumb,
Glancing around at the strange room.
Nothing, Ludmila, in this chamber
Matches at all what you remember.
You're floating on a feather bed
Under a costly canopy,
The curtains, fabrics, you can see
Are all embossed with rich brocade;
Gems glow like fire; silk cloths present
Scenes lyrical or scenes dramatic;
Gold censers waft an aromatic
And hazy mist that's clearly meant
To soothe yet stir up ... But enough:
Someone's described this kind of stuff
Long before me: Scheherazade.
I couldn't measure up to her;
Besides, the finest bedroom's sad,
Lacking the lover you prefer.

*

Three maids, each like a charming fairy,
In raiment lovely, light and airy,
Come gliding in without a sound
And make a full bow, to the ground.
One tiptoes close to her, and lingers,
With gestures making her aware
She wishes, with ethereal fingers,
To plait Ludmila's golden hair,
And starts to do so, in a way
Considered out of date today,
Setting a circlet of fine pearl
Upon the brow of the pale girl.
A second maiden, her gaze lowered,
Respectful, modest, then glides forward,
Adroitly slides a blue silk gown
Over her head and smooths it down;
And over that, from crown to breast,
A veil diaphanous as mist.
The garments show the figure under,
A beauty less of earth than heaven;
Exquisite shoes embellish even
Her dainty, naked feet – a wonder.
She moves away, and the third maiden
Brings her a sash with pearls ablaze.
And all this time a singer, hidden,

Sings for her lays of joy and praise.
Alas, the raiment so luxurious,
The songs a sweet voice nearby sings,
All the seductive ritual, brings
No pleasure. She's not even curious
When asked to look into a mirror
And marvel at her new costume:
Her feelings she could not make clearer,
Dropping her gaze, is speechless, numb.
He who most often turns the leaves
Of the heart's book, known to its core,
Yet of some girl is still unsure
She mourns as much as she believes
For an unhappy, lost amour,
Or a romantic tale she weaves:
Does she neglect her mirror? For
Ignoring mirrors means she grieves.

Now she is left alone and lonely.
Entirely lost for what to do,
Walks to the window and looks through
Its lattice screen. She can see only
A landscape dreary beyond measure,
Everything dead. Nothing but snow

Carpeting plains which stretch below,
And peaks of mountains which oppress her:
The sombre white that's taken hold,
Their slumber in eternal cold.
No chimney smoke marks out a pleasant
Cottage; no merry hunting horn
Resounds among the slopes forlorn;
Not even a homeward-trudging peasant;
No movement and no sound are present,
But only, now and then, a wind
Whimpers or wails, now sharp,
     now thinned,
And merging into the sky's drab grey
The bleak, denuded forests sway.

Face in her hands, she let her tears
Flow freely, overwhelmed by fears
Of horrors that might be in store.
She scurried to a silver door.
It opened with a pleasing sound,
Some chords of music, then she found
Herself in gardens more enchanting
Than those in which Armida held
The knight Rinaldo captive, planting

Love in his heart, by love impelled.
Before Ludmila rustle and roar
Great groves of trees in all their splendour;
Palm alleys, paths where myrtles render
Their tender scent; proud cedars soar;
A wood of bays the princess sees,
Then lushly golden orange trees;
Hillocks and copses, vales and leas
By springtime's blaze are resurrected,
Fresh blows the cooling breeze of May;
Amid this spellbound, later Eden
A nightingale sings her dulcet lay,
Deep in a wood's recesses hidden;
Spray from great fountains rising, falling,
Refreshes moss, and fern, and grass,
And marble statues, standing, sprawling,
So much alive that Phidias,
Though taught by Pallas and Apollo,
Could he but look at them would throw
Away his chisel, grieving, know
Compared to these his work was hollow.
Tall waterfalls are splashing, sparkling,
Creating sunny, jewelled arcs,
While not far off, in woodlands darkling,
Only the faintest plashing marks

The hiding place of sleepy brooks.
Greenness abounds, but here and there,
Havens for coolness, rest and quiet,
Splashes of brilliant white declare
A summer house. Around, a riot
Of crimson roses scents the air.
But nothing solaces Ludmila;
She walks and walks, yet does not see;
The sensuous splendour does not thrill her,
Deepens indeed her misery;
Whither she does not know, she wanders,
Circles the garden, then meanders,
Continuing all the way to weep;
Her eyes look up, and prayers she tenders
To the kind gods there, but they sleep.
But suddenly her face is radiant,
A finger presses on her teeth
From glee: a dread thought underneath
Has surfaced . . . Just one awesome gradient
Away is peace . . . Above a torrent
A high bridge swings from cliff to cliff.
Here is a way to end all grief,
To end a life become abhorrent.
The waters boil as in a fever
Below; sobbing, she strikes her breast,

Resolved to jump, and there find rest.
She did not take that leap, however,
But to the other cliff she crossed.

And soon, my wonderful Ludmila,
Seeing the sun to midday climb,
Felt tiredness weigh her feet then fill her;
Drying her eyes she thought, It's time!
She sat down on the grass, and lo!
Around her is a tent, cool, shady,
And food and drink in plenty flow,
A feast appropriate to a lady,
By crystal charmingly displayed;
And like a distant waterfall
Sweet music on a harp is played,
Enthralling the princess in thrall.
But as sweet fumes and music swirled,
She thought, 'It's all a masquerade;
Why longer stay in this vile world,
Torn from my love? You whose desire
Is dark, torment with luxury,
But I fear not your wicked power:
Ludmila knows the way to die!
You do not tempt me in the least

With tedious music and this feast;
I'll fast to death: no mead, no meat,
Shall pass my lips till life has ceased . . .'
And with these thoughts – begins to eat.

The princess stands; at once the spacious
Tent, what remains of the delicious
Repast, the opulent tableware,
The harp song, vanish into thin air.
Again she's in the garden walking,
Slowly she moves from grove to grove.
Meanwhile, in darkening skies above,
The moon, the queen of night, is stalking,
Into the garden soft mists creep,
To drowse on shrubs and trees and gorse;
Ludmila too can barely keep
Her eyes wide open. Then some force
Lifts her as gently as a breeze,
Bears her as gently, then composes
Her form, in manner sure to please
Whoever scents this room with roses,
On the same bed, her bed of tears.
Now the same trinity appears;
All three start busily undressing

The girl, at hooks their fingers fly,
But now their faces are expressing
A bleakness, a despondency;
And in their silent offering
They hint at fellow suffering,
A helpless, sullen rage at fate.
Let's move more quickly: by their tender,
Swift ministrations she's stripped bare,
Then clad in a white shift to render
– So artlessly it clings to her –
Her loveliness still lovelier.
She lies down. The three maidens bow,
Sighing, then scurry to the door
Which opens quietly. What now?
The exhausted girl catnaps a moment,
Then, doubly attentive, concentrates,
Her fearful eyes and mind in ferment,
On searching blackness . . . for what waits.
She trembles, lies in silence, rigid,
And hears thud, under her thin garment,
Her heart. She cannot feel her frigid
Fingers. Now silence . . . whispering!
She hides in pillows now her head,
For *it* is moving towards her bed.
What terror can a whisper bring

In the dark night! And it's well-founded:
The door is opened and light flares,
And she is frightened and confounded
By sight of Moors, arranged in pairs,
A long procession; proud their bearing,
Light on their naked sabres flaring;
On tiny cushions is a weird
Something that's clearly valued greatly,
So careful are they – a grey beard.
Behind it walks, sedate and stately,
A hunchbacked dwarf, chin-high. It is
To him the beard belongs. His skull,
Hairless, is hidden by a tall
– What call it? – skullcap, tarboosh, fez.
He's moved up close, and with a swoosh
The girl is out of bed and shaking
Her fist at him; grasps his tarboosh
Or fez, and is so loudly shrieking
The Moors are deafened, and the dwarf
Turns paler than his frantic captive,
Staggers, his feet entangled in
His beard, attempting to run off,
And falls; confused, the maladaptive
Moors chatter; he stands and falls again;
A Moor with one arm sweeps him up,

Untangling the long beard, so treasured;
They run out with the stunted wizard,
Leaving her holding his skullcap.

We left Ruslan, at nightfall, waiting.
Take up, Orlovsky, your swift pencil
And sketch that unexpected meeting
Of knights not bent on friendly counsel.

Already a faint moon appears.
The fight is savage and intense,
Both boil with rage and violence;
Far distant from them lie their spears,
Both swords have long ago been shattered,
Their shields too; armour, blood-bespattered.
Their horses join the deadly joust,
Kicking up skywards a black dust.
Rider and horse each like a centaur,
The steel-clad fighters interlace,
Such hatred there no light can enter;
Helms mask each boiling, blood-red face,
Breast against breast, a crazed embrace.
At last, though, both of them are weakening,

Their grip upon each other slackening;
Now Ruslan, rage-filled, with one heave
Forces the other knight to leave
His saddle, then, intent on slaughter,
Lifts him and holds, with iron fist,
Then flings him to the rocks and water
Below, and shouts, 'There is your tryst –
With death, not my Ludmila! Die
And rot there with your jealousy!'

Dear reader, I am much astray if
You have not guessed who that knight was:
Eager for any blood-soaked cause,
It was Rogdai, the hope of Kiev.
He'd tracked along the Dnieper's banks
The footprints of Ruslan, and thanks
To his sharp eyes and his persistence
Had found the prince. But to what use?
Strength against fate has no resistance,
And he, the darling of old Rus',
Discovered even he could lose.
Along the Dnieper the tale lingers,
And I have often heard it sung
Around a campfire, that a young

Rusalka took, with her cold fingers,
Rogdai down into the black deeps,
Laughing, and with caresses keeps
Him there. When, dank and cold and cheerless,
Darkness upon the river falls,
Over the ages, now and then
The dreadful ghost of the once fearless
Warrior frightens and appals
The huddled Dnieper fishermen.

CANTO THREE

Cold sunlight was already gilding
The peak where the dwarf's castle stood,
But gloomy silence filled the building,
From dread at Chernomor's vile mood,
Sitting up on his bed, and yawning,
Capless and in his dressing gown.
Around him his black slaves were fawning,
And with a comb of fine ox bone
Smoothed out and styled his beard, and snipped
Off stragglers as he sat grim-lipped.
Meanwhile they rubbed with sweating palms
Luxurious oriental balms
Into his whiskers which grew wildly

And used the curling irons, mildly.
Then suddenly through the window sails
A dragon, clanging its iron scales,
Turns into circles for a fleeting
Moment, and then becomes the crone
Naïna, amazing everyone.
Her old voice croaks, 'I give you greeting!
Brother, your fame I have long known,
So scarcely view you as a stranger;
To meet you now – well, I feel proud;
My dear, we face a common danger;
Wise Chernomor, a threatening cloud
Hangs over you; and over me
An insult – my honour has been slighted.
We face the selfsame enmity;
My hope is, we shall stand united.'

He fixed on her his crafty gaze
And offered his small hand. 'Delighted!
And likewise I've heard only praise
For you; and yes, we'll stand united
Against the traps the Finn has baited.
But I don't fear his cunning ploys;
His power, Naïna, is not great.

Listen: I have been blessed by fate;
This beard, though it looks soft and gentle,
Is mighty, not merely ornamental;
Unless a hostile sword can sever
This beard, no knight, alive or dead,
Can alter by a single thread
My plans; Ludmila's mine forever.
Ruslan? His death he can't resist.'
She shrieked: 'He's going to perish! Perish!'
Stamped three times, and then three times hissed,
Became a dragon with a flourish,
And flew off in a vengeful mist.

Dressed in a garment sumptuous, garish,
The wizard, by the sorceress cheered,
Decided he would take his beard,
Respect and love – all three effective –
This time to win his lovely captive.
If he'd offended he'd ask pardon.
He goes ... Around her room he hurtles ...
Princess there's none. Out to the garden,
The park, and the paths lined with myrtles,
The lakes, the groves, the waterfalls,
The bridge, the summer houses ... gone!

He tries to run, but trips, and sprawls.
Imagine his humiliation,
His grief, his frantic agitation!
He scarcely sees the light of day.
Now, summoning his slaves, he calls:
'You rascals, come and help your master!
Ludmila, she has run away!
You wretched layabouts, run faster!
And if you're playing a bad joke
On me, the lot of you will croak!'

We left Ludmila in a state
Of agitation. What thereafter?
All night she wondered at her fate
And wept, but there was also laughter.
The beard had frightened her; however,
She had faced Chernomor, and found
Him clownish, and with shudders never
Can giggling fits find common ground.
She rose from bed at dawning light
And, as she'd done since first she grew
To lovely girlhood, turned to view
Herself reflected, lofty, bright,
And with the same instinctive action

Moved from her shoulders, lily-white,
Tresses so powerful an attraction,
Then plaited her luxuriant flaxen
Hair by long habit, her hands flying.
She found last night's clothes in a corner,
And, dressing, began again to mourn her
Sad plight; she started gently crying.
Still on the mirror kept her gaze,
And suddenly a quite delicious
Idea sprang, for a girl's ways
Are often charmingly capricious:
Chernomor's cap, why not try on!
She is alone here, viewed by none,
She's seventeen, pretty, and no matter
What hat she puts on, it will flatter;
Dressing up's fun, a lady's fetish!
A dozen styles the girl unfurls:
Straight, over her brow, showing her curls,
Then tilts it, so it looks coquettish;
Finally back to front she twirls
The hat and – wonder of ancient days!
Ludmila's vanished from the mirror;
Rightens the cap – and in her gaze
Ludmila's gazing, never clearer;
Turns back to front – she's gone again.

She sits – her image too! 'It's brilliant!
O thank you, wizard, thank you, light!
I proved last night I was resilient,
And so you're making plans to smite
The awkward hussy – but you can't!'
From joy the girl began to blush,
And firmly planted back to front
The wizard's cap, fez or tarboosh.

Let's leave her in a happy state;
Enough of hats and beards and suchlike
Or you will think that I too much like
Trivia: let's turn to Ruslan's fate.
He, having overcome Rogdai,
Travels a sombre woodland trail,
Then finds himself in a broad vale
Just as bright morning lights the sky.
He shivers: before him, stretching far,
The relics of an ancient war.
Gleam yellow bones around the field,
A bow, a breastplate, rusted shield;
A ribcage, with a blade run through it;
Here lies an ancient harness, here
A helm with weeds and hairs stuck to it,

The skull it once held lying near . . .
A knight posed as if action lingers,
As if for courage there's still need,
His rusted sword in bony fingers,
Still seated on his bony steed . . .
Ivy-entwined, from earth protruding,
Arrows, lances . . . Peacefulness
And an eternal silence brooding
On the untroubled wilderness,
Only the brilliant sun intruding
On doleful leas the dead possess.

Ruslan looks all around the meadow,
Grieving, imagining the groans
And screams. 'O vale of death, who sowed you
With sterile seed, these endless bones?
Whose swift horse at the latest hour
Of battle trampled on you still?
Who implored heaven with his prayer?
Who deserved fame, but alas fell?
Why are you silent as your grass,
Adding oblivion to starkness? . . .
And possibly I too shall pass
In such a way into the darkness!

Perhaps some hill where silence reigns
Shall hold Ruslan's grave, unknown, grim,
And never shall Bayan's sweet strains
Utter a word of praise for him!'
But swiftly stronger thoughts prevail;
He needs a trusty sword; no less
Desirable, a coat of mail,
Being vulnerable and weaponless,
So much by Rogdai had been shattered.
A purpose bringing greater calm,
He looks, amid the mouldering, scattered
Bones for a sword, some armour, helm.
The clatter as he kicks at metals
Eerily wakes the sleeping field
A moment, then to sleep it settles
Once more. He picks up helm and shield,
But the right sword remains concealed.
He has examined a whole medley,
But they are too light or too small
For one of princely strength, though sadly
Today's knights would have liked them all.
Bored now, he grasps a lance that's faced
Many a battle, many a tourney,
Then puts an hauberk on his chest,
And so re-armed, resumes his journey.

*

Fades the red sunset into pallor,
And blue-grey mists are settling on
The sleepy earth; then one bright colour
Comes swimming up, the golden moon;
The steppes are dim, on darkened grasses
Pensively travels our Ruslan;
And sees, as through night's murk he passes,
A mound, of monstrous height and span,
And hears what seems a monstrous snore.
Closer . . . as man and horse come near it
Ruslan is certain – you can hear it!
The mound is breathing! While he's more
Alert, he does not yield to fears;
His horse, however, pricks back its ears,
Quivers, as if it's seen a spirit,
Tosses its mane, whinnies, rears up.
In transient moonlight now appears
The mound lit up from base to top.
Ruslan sees – all my words have fled
As it's so weird! – a living head.
It sleeps, its eyelids giant shutters,
And every snore it thunders flutters
Skywards its helmet's lofty plume,

While feathers from it float and, fading,
Fall earthwards. In its monstrous gloom
It bars the way to hosts invading
This nameless plain. Confused, perplexed,
And with its wondrousness quite taken,
Ruslan conceives a wish to waken
The head. First, gazes keenly; next,
He rides around it; ponders on
The nose; the nostrils with his lance he teases;
They wrinkle, crinkle up . . . a yawn;
The eyes flash open, and it sneezes!
The plain shakes and a whirlwind howls,
Clouds of dust rise; the whiskers, ears,
Eyebrows release a flock of owls;
Awaken all the groves from sleep;
The sneeze re-echoes, the horse rears
And bucks, so he can hardly keep
His seat; and then the huge mouth thundered:
'What impudence! By God, you've blundered!
Turn back, knight, or this day you'll rue:
I gobble brazen fools like you!'
Prince Ruslan, sharply reining in
His horse, was silent, offering merely
A long stare, then disdainful grin.
Taken aback, the head in surly

Tones muttered, 'What do you want of me?
Such fools I'm sent by destiny!
Listen to what I'm saying: piss off!
I want to sleep, my space you're crowding.'
In face of this, so coarse, abrasive,
The proud prince answers, his face clouding:
'Our fathers did not say in vain,
Bigger the skull, smaller the brain!
In peace I ride on, but take care you
Don't try to stop me: I won't spare you.'

At this, the head begins to swell
Until it is completely bloated;
The eyes with flames begin to roll,
Lips pale, as if with chalk dust coated,
So tightly wound up is its fury;
And from its mouth hot steam and slurry
Comes spewing forth – and as it flows,
The head, cheeks puffed, at Ruslan blows.
And now the horse, its eyes shut tight,
Head lowered, and chest heaving, straining,
Charged off through whirlwind, rain and night,
With no intention of remaining,
Careering in its wayward flight,

Stricken with terror and half-blinded,
Strength drained away but single-minded.
Its rider tried with all his might
To turn around his rampant steed,
But fruitlessly – the horse decreed!
After them flew the head gigantic,
Now cackling like a lunatic
And roaring, 'Hero, why so frantic?
Fleeing like that, you'll break your neck!
Don't be so lily-livered: stop,
Before your nag decides to drop!
Come, try to hit me – be courageous!'
Ruslan was boiling with vexation,
And when a tongue, immense, outrageous,
Poked out, in added provocation,
The knight drew back his spear and flung
It full force, saw it pierce, vibrate,
In that obscene, insulting tongue.
Thence like a river in full spate
The blood gushed forth. The head, amazed,
Gnawing on steel, gone all bravado,
For several moments merely gazed
In shock, the face grey as a shadow,
Showing a sickly, baffled rage;
As when an actor, talent missing,

Hamming his tragic lines on stage,
Is deafened by a sudden hissing
And whistling, and he pales from fright,
The auditorium black as night,
And all his lines he has forgot;
He trembles, drops his head, and stammers,
His confidence completely shot
As 'Off!' the laughing darkness clamours.
The advantage of a moment seizing,
The head confused, its actions freezing,
Our warrior raised and swung his hand
Clad in its heavy gauntlet, and
Struck the head's cheek with hawklike speed,
So hard, the blow reverberated
Around the plain, and the blood spouted,
Sowing the grass as if with seed,
Turning dew crimson. The head, tottering,
Tried to stay up, tipped over and rolled,
Its helm bouncing along and clattering.
Ruslan saw, glittering with gold,
Where hitherto the head had been,
A sword, the kind a prince would hold,
A warrior's sword. No sooner seen
Than seized; with tremulous joy he ran,
His heart now boiling in dark throes

Of bloodlust, over the blood-covered
Grass, to cut off the ears and nose
Of the stunned head. His broad sword hovered,
About to cut; but then he heard,
Amazed, a voice for mercy pleading,
A humble voice; he drops his sword,
The lust to hurt at once receding,
The gentler feelings in him rally,
His frenzied anger is all gone;
As ice that lingers in a valley
Melts at the touch of midday sun.

'Good knight, you've brought me to my senses,'
Sighing, the head said. 'To my shame
It took the blows your hand dispenses
To realise I was to blame.
I'll try your trust henceforth to merit,
And ask you to be great in spirit.
Worthy of pity is my fate;
I was myself a valiant knight;
Many the knight forced to importune
Me to be merciful. My life
Was happy – but for the misfortune
Of having a jealous, cunning dwarf

As brother; his name, Chernomor.
You, Chernomor! source of my ruin,
Whom all our kindred folk abhor;
Born stunted, bearded; with him flew in
A thousand devils to torment me;
My greater height from his first days
He saw, and started to resent me,
And looked for sly, inhuman ways
To pay me out. I'm – well, not daft,
But simple, while he's devilish smart
And knows of evil the black art,
This midget at whom people laughed.
And you should know that, to my ill,
That beard of his holds magic power,
Can make the whole wide world cower,
And so long as that beard stays whole
He fears no one, is in control.
He came to me one day pretending
A brotherly goodwill, and said:
"Please listen: we both need defending,
For in the dark books I have read
Where eastern peaks so steeply rise
The seas below are scarcely heard,
In a deep-buried vault there lies
– I shudder saying it! – a sword;

And I have learned through my long study
That when unfriendly fate is ready
That sword is meant to strike us dead,
I losing beard, and you your head.
So it is vital we acquire it;
A hard task, lighter if we've shared
The burden of it: can you bear it?"
– "I'm with you, brother," I declared;
"If need be, the whole world searching."
On my right shoulder perched my brother,
To guide me, said he, as I strode,
And a pine branch was on the other.
We set off on the long, long road.
At first God's blessings fell like fountains,
As if to spite the prophecy;
We found the mighty eastern mountains
And, lapping them, the quiet sea;
My brother's skill I could not fault,
We even found the fateful vault.
I groped on hands and knees around it,
Seeking the sword, and at last found it.
There good luck ended; fate unfurled
Its dark intentions: we two quarrelled.
What shattered our unreal accord?
The question was, who owned the sword?

For hours we argued; finally,
Switching to the mild voice of reason,
But really plotting secret treason,
The dwarf proposed a remedy.
"Let's stop this rowing – it's a bore,"
Gravely suggested Chernomor.
"We need to reach an understanding;
We have become quite close of late
And we can keep that bond by handing
The question we dispute to fate.
Let's lay our ears close to the ground,
And he who first hears (akh, that knave!)
Out of the earth a ringing sound
Shall own the weapon to the grave."
With that, he lay flat, and I duly
Stretched out, although I knew the nature
Of that most loathsome, treacherous creature,
So I can only blame my folly.
No ringing sound, of course, I heard,
Nor could I hear him stand and steal
Up behind me – nothing, till
I heard the swish of the sharp sword;
And even as I glanced around
My head lay severed; yet I found
That through some supernatural force

It keeps the breath of life, alas.
My manly trunk my brother carried
To where no one will mourn for me,
Far off; beneath a blackthorn tree
It lies now, rotting and unburied.
The dwarf brought me, my living part,
Unto this dismal place, to guard
Eternally the magic sword.
Fate wants you to possess it, knight:
A good man ought to be its rightful
Owner. God bless you on your road,
And if you meet that murderous, frightful
Ogre you'll earn my gratitude
By smiting him! For only thus
Can I cast off the spell that's held me
To memories of treachery
Tormenting, leave this world in peace,
Forget all – even your blow that felled me.'

CANTO FOUR

I never cease the Lord to praise
Each morning when I wake from slumber
That in these more prosaic days
Magicians have declined in number.
Those that remain – let's honour them –
Aren't so unkind as to imperil,
With knavish spell or stratagem,
The nuptial night of lad and girl.
I do, though, fear a new variety
Of witchcraft, for it makes me wilt:
Sweet blue eyes flashing in society,
The enchanting smile, a voice's lilt.
Be wary, friends, of the elation

Evoked by them: their aim is strife,
A poisonous intoxication;
Shun them, and lead a quiet life.

Friends, you have often heard the tale
Of an old sinner's wicked sale
Of his own soul then, asked for more,
His daughters' souls to Lucifer.
Then how, through charitable giving,
The prayers and fasts that faith decreed,
And altogether holy living,
He found a saint to intercede;
How his twelve daughters slept, enchanted,
Which brought us terror and delight,
By the still-sleeping maidens haunted.
We'd share the tale – then dream at night.
Once we'd been frightened by God's wrath,
We youthful comrades were not loath
To dwell on maids whose lives were
        squandered;
We wept with them, with them we wandered
Around the castle's walls and keep,
And joined their quiet, captive sleep;
We called on Vadim's soul to wake them,

These innocents with untouched breasts
We were in love with, and he'd take them
Often to where their father rests.
But could it be the legend lied?
Could I be a more truthful guide? . . .

Ratmir, the Khazar Khan, directed
His swift steed southwards, and expected
Before the day's last glimmers died
To have Ludmila by his side,
While Ruslan, Rogdai and Farlaf,
On wild goose chases, would sleep rough.
But crimson skies, as the sun lowered,
Were darkened by a mist, until
However hard his sight strained forward
Beyond the river, murky, chill,
He could not see. Some rays broke
    through,
Flaming a wood with gold; that light
Showed steepling rocks, and Ratmir knew
He must find shelter for the night.
But suddenly he rides beneath
A steepling crag, and thereupon
A castle's walls like jagged teeth;

And there, a maiden, like a swan
Gliding alone on waters, walks
And sings, the last of sunset glistening
On her and, his ears straining, listening
Is Ratmir, far below the rocks.

'It's late; bitter the dark wood;
The sea winds bring in sharp hail showers;
Traveller, you with your young blood,
Find comfort in this home of ours.

We offer gentle slumber here,
On a fine feather bed; and after
You wake, you will find feasts and laughter
With us: O come, young traveller!

You will find lovely damsels here,
With tender speech and lips delightful;
Come to our secret call this nightfall,
Rise up to us, young traveller!

When the first rays of sun appear
We'll fill a cup that's warming, cheerful;
We call in peace, do not be fearful
But come to us, young traveller!

It's late; bitter the dark wood;
The sea winds bring in sharp hail showers;
Traveller, you with your young blood,
Find comfort in this home of ours.'

She sings to him, her voice caressing,
As underneath the walls he stands,
Then at the gates are girls expressing
Their welcome with soft outstretched
        hands;
There's girlish chatter in a circle
Around him, and he feels the force
Of eyes that, gazing on him, sparkle;
Two maidens lead away his horse;
Another to his chamber lights
The way; more lovely anchorites
Follow; one takes his helm and spear as
Another girl removes his cuirass;

Removed too is his dusty shield;
The iron plates of war must yield
To softer clothes. But first he's brought
To a bath house of Russian splendour;
Already water, steaming hot
Fills silver tubs, and fountains render
A spray of cooling, breezy freshness;
On fine rugs with a springy lushness
The weary Khan lies down, and steam,
Wispy, transparent, plays on him.
Young beauties, mute, in half-undress,
All seeing more than it would seem
From eyes demurely lowered, press
Around and tenderly caress
His body, playful. One is waving
Birch twigs above him, which produce
A warm sensation; one is laving
Him with fresh roses, whose spring juice
Cools his tired body and makes fragrant
With its aroma his dark curls.
Drunk on the beauty of these girls,
Their touches feeding a swift fire,
His former feelings have turned vagrant:
That longing, that pent-up desire,
To have Ludmila, and his duty

To the old Prince – forgotten, all!
With roving eyes he is in thrall
To now one, now another, beauty.
He flames more with each new sensation,
And his heart thrills with expectation.

In velvets suited to a noble
Having been dressed, and to a table
Led by these wondrous girls, Ratmir
Sees a most splendid feast appear.
I don't possess the gift of Homer
Whose soaring verses were at home
With warriors' lengthy feasts, the foam
And crash of goblets, and the clamour;
I, recklessly, in Parny's steps,
Prefer to show some slender damsel
When fall of dark is a preamble
To soft, bared flesh and tender lips!
The castle in soft moonlight gleams;
I see the dim, secluded chamber
Where the knight, tired in every member,
Deeply aroused still, sleeps and dreams;
His cheeks are crimson as a rose,
Torso and limbs are likewise burning;

Half-open lips prepare to close
On lips that equally are yearning;
He sighs at kisses' brief cessation,
Seeing what no words can express;
The quilt's clasped to his breast with passion.
But now, in the deep quietness,
The door is opened; as though jealous
The floor squeaks under light, quick, zealous
Footsteps. Flits in, in moonlight's dress,
No more, a girl. Dearest, awaken!
Spread wide, you wings of sleep, begone!
Awaken, love, the night is done!
Lost is the moment if not taken!
Closer, up to the bed, she creeps,
He in voluptuous pleasure sleeps;
From off the bed the cover slides,
Into warm pillows he subsides.
Holding her breath now she leans over
His handsome form, deprived of cover,
Imagining his touch upon her
Like chastely libertine Diana
Gazing down at her shepherd lad.
Sighing, one knee upon the bed,
She tries, as only young girls can,
Trembling, by violent feelings shaken,

With passionate kisses to awaken
The dream-excited Khazar Khan . . .

But now, my friends, I must lay by
My virgin lyre; its sounds appear
Shakier somehow, since I'm shy;
We'll have to leave there young Ratmir –
I need some time out to recover,
And Ruslan we have long withheld,
Ruslan, that knight unparalleled,
Heroic soul, truehearted lover.
Under a head – a strange arrangement –
Exhausted by the grim engagement
He sleeps until the break of day,
Sunlight in frolicsome engagement
With the head's hair in disarray,
Tinting the thick black locks with gold.
Ruslan stands up; though stiff and cold,
Mounts his bold horse and is away.

The days flash by; the fields turn yellow;
Wind sends the autumn woodlands rustling,
And drowns out songbirds with its whistling;

Day after day leaves thin and sallow
Float down, although he barely sees
The nearest bare, bedraggled trees;
Winter is nearing – but Ruslan
Maintains the course he settled on,
To the far north; though every day
Something or other blocks his way:
Now it's another knight, defiant,
Now a sly witch, and now a giant;
And once, when he is fog-enshrouded,
The only gleam the murky, dim
Light of the moon, as in a dream
He meets a shoal of mermaids, crowded
On a tree's branches, tempting him
With wicked smiles to go with them;
But faithful to the fate he chose,
Ruslan rides by, he does not see them,
His drum beats to a different rhythm,
Always Ludmila with him goes.

But in the meantime, unobserved,
Having the dwarf's cap to conceal her,
From his grotesque assaults preserved,
What's happening to my Ludmila,

To my adorable princess?
Silently, in profound distress,
She wanders aimless round the garden,
Grief for Ruslan a heavy burden.
Often to dreaminess she yields
And is back home in Kiev's fields,
With friends, her father and her brothers,
Her nurses, all like loving mothers;
Forgotten is the separation.
But suddenly her dreams are gone,
And with them her imagination –
She's here, unhappy and alone.
Meanwhile the dwarf's black cohorts bustle
Around the gardens and the castle,
By day and night, in search of her;
Enraged they shout her name, and swear;
And now and then the girl will hassle
Them further with an apparition
In one of the enchanted groves,
Her cap off, calling in derision,
'I'm here, I'm here!' Then swiftly moves,
Invisible again, as their
Rapacious hands are clutching air.
They saw, and angrily remarked on,
Signs of her presence everywhere:

Some ripe fruit picked, a branch now bare,
Peel from an orange she has sucked on;
Or they see splashes of spring water
On lawns that ought to be bone-dry:
For food and drink she can rely
On ways a homely nurse once taught her.
A cedar or a birch will serve her
At night as a safe resting place,
But mostly tears run down her face;
She calls her love with anguished fervour,
Yawning from tiredness and depression;
And rarely, rarely, before dawn
Does true sleep come and take possession;
She drowses briefly, like a swan;
And while the dawn light is still dim
She to a waterfall's cold stream;
The dwarf once, from his chamber window,
Saw falling water rise and spray
Repetitively, like a rondeau,
As if unseen hands were at play.
After her bathe, all day she wandered,
Hands to her face in her despair,
Around the lawns and groves meandered;
And often, on the evening air,
Her small, sweet voice could be heard singing;

Often a slave would hasten, bringing
Some sign of her she had let fall,
A handkerchief with her tears wringing,
A nimbly woven coronal
Of flowers, threads from a Persian shawl.

Boiling with injured pride and spite,
The dwarf in his dark mind was busy
Considering ways by which he might
Entrap this tease, this trull, this hussy.
Recall Hephaestus, the lame smith,
With Aphrodite wed till death,
A net of steel and gold designed
To trap her naked with her lover;
The gods took ages to recover
From laughs at Love and War entwined.

One day, bored and her mind straying,
In a cool marble summer house
She gazed out mournfully through swaying
Branches at a lawn riotous
With flowers in bloom, and her heart stilled,
Hearing, 'My love!', and saw Ruslan

Indeed, his features, bearing, build;
But he looked dull of eye and wan,
And on his thigh a wound. Now sorrow
Makes her heart shudder; she cries out,
'Ruslan! Ruslan!' without a doubt
That it is he, and like an arrow
Is out the door ... tears, a whole storm:
'You're here ... You're hurt ... Lord give me faith!'
Runs to embrace his lovely form,
Holds – nothing! Horror ... gone, that wraith!
A mesh about her body's wound
And her cap's fallen to the ground.
She turns as cold as though a blizzard
Blew through the garden trees, and hears
A shout, 'She's mine!' ring in her ears
Above her whimper; as the wizard
Appears, she falls; and now sleep brings
Peace with its warm, enfolding wings.

Now what will happen to Ludmila?
Seeing her helpless lying there
The dwarf lays reechy hands on her;
But will it be enough to feel her
Soft body? From his lust and rage,

Not so. But suddenly the shrill
Call of a horn, and the shocked mage
Turns pale: does someone mean him ill?
The horn rings out still louder, bolder!
He slaps the cap back on the girl
And flies to meet the unknown churl,
His long beard streaming past his shoulder.

CANTO FIVE

But who has set the horn resounding,
Challenged the wizard to confront him,
His dissolute assault confounding?
Ruslan. He's traced at last the phantom
Who stole his love, and thirsts to wreak
Vengeance on him. He stands below
The castle walls, and his horn's shriek
Frightens his steed, it paws the snow.
Then as it were a bolt of thunder
Falls on his helmet of stern steel
Hurting the skull so fragile under,
And makes the doughty warrior reel.
His dazed eyes gaze at what before

He's had in nightmares to imagine,
The dwarfish form of Chernomor,
With an upraised, enormous bludgeon,
Floating above. His shield Ruslan
Upraises, waves his sword, but sees
Chernomor rising, hid in haze,
One second there, the next he's gone –
Now from on high comes charging down.
Ruslan, though, with a deft manoeuvre,
Evades; the mage into packed snow
Smashes, and lies stunned by the blow;
Ruslan, before he can recover,
Was off his steed, with one stride cleared
The ground between, and by his beard
Got hold of him. He groaned and strained,
And with Ruslan was skyward flying,
Leaving a horse astonished, eyeing
Its master as he rose and waned;
Never was a sight so weird,
Its master clinging by a beard!
They fly, in whirls Ruslan finds sickening,
Over dark forest, sunlit vale,
Over harsh mountains now they sail,
Now stormy seas, speed ever quickening,
The prince's grip from tiredness weakening,

He fears each moment it must fail.
But this the wizard does not know
And, tired himself, begins to slow;
He gasps out: 'This could end in murder;
I don't want that, I'll let you live,
As I admire your youthful ardour;
I'll forget all, and all forgive;
I'll land us – but on one condition . . .'
'Silence, you wicked sorcerer!' –
Ruslan breaks in – 'No buts I'll hear;
Wife-stealer, you're in no position
To bargain; I've my trusty sword;
Up to the stars I don't mind flying –
But you will be without your beard!'
From fright the dwarf thinks he is dying;
Tugs at his beard to move it clear
And send this villain into orbit . . .
No good; with humour slightly morbid
The knight even plucks out the odd hair.
Two days and nights they fly, till Vega's
Light is quite blinding; then the magus,
His looming face as pale as death:
'You've won, Prince; I can scarce find
        breath;
Just spare my life, and take whatever

You wish . . .' – 'You yield to Russian valour?
You're done for, eh? . . . Ah yes, you shiver!
Now carry me to my Ludmila.'

All his resistance having crumbled,
Chernomor flew and in a trice
The moutains of his realm of ice
Appeared, and into snow they tumbled.
Then Ruslan with the sword the head
Had passed to him, seizing the dwarf
With his free hand, cut his beard off
Like weeds scythed from a flower bed.
'You're ours, knave!' he cried out. 'Now savour
How you are weakened and disgraced!'
With that, upon his helm he placed
The grey beard like a lady's favour;
He whistled, calling his brave steed,
Who flew to him: the master's back!
The wizard, too half-dead to plead,
Was stuffed into his saddle pack.
He himself bounded up the steep
Pathway to the magician's keep,
Joy made his progress swift and nimble;
He enters, on his helm the symbol

Of having overcome the mage;
Then fearful inmates of this prison,
Moors, maids, a momentary vision,
Appear – then vanish from the stage.
He strides from empty hall to hall
Calling Ludmila's name; but solely
His voice, more and more melancholy,
Echoes to him his loving call.
Increasingly disturbed in mind,
He finds the garden door, then searches
The groves, the copses, tree-lined arches –
Nowhere Ludmila can he find.
The waterfall, the summer houses,
Rivers and cliffs ... Everything's dead;
He hearkens for her voice; instead,
The kind of sleep that nothing rouses.
A sudden chill takes hold of him
And in his eyes the light has darkened
And in his mind there's only gloom ...
'Perhaps ... that monster left his mark, and
Despair and shame ... One moment ... river ...'
He's desolate, hangs low his head,
Standing transfixed, with not a quiver,
Like a tall stone that marks the dead.
A darkness clouds his very reason,

Wild flames around his body move,
And through his veins there runs the poison
Of frantic and despairing love.
It seems . . . the shadow of her slips
Out of the trees, her tremulous lips
Are pressed to his . . . And now he bounds
In a mad rage around the grounds,
Over and over 'Ludmila!' wailing,
Lifts rocks from crags and sends them rolling,
He hacks and slashes with his sword,
Pavilions, whole arcades, come crashing,
Plants lie around the ravaged sward,
Bridges are into gullies smashing;
His mighty sabre sings and whistles,
The garden's loveliness is gone,
Tall oaks and marble statues shatter,
And far and wide beyond the castle's
Walls resound roar and clash and groan –
The crazed knight is hellbent on slaughter,
To left and right in fury swings,
A war with thin air often waging.
And one such slash by pure chance brings,
Through the magician's cap dislodging,
A wondrous sight . . . Ludmila lies
Before him, tangled in a net.

At first he can't believe his eyes,
So without hope he fears to let
Joy in. But now he kneels before her,
His true love, his delight, his bride;
Slashes her free; his hot tears slide,
Kisses her, calls her, to restore her –
For the princess is sleeping; sight
Is blind, and hearing deaf, to him,
She's dreaming her untroubled dream,
Her young breasts' rise and fall is slight.
Ruslan's gaze never leaves her face;
Another torture now begins ...
But suddenly another voice,
A voice familiar, kind: the Finn's:

'Take heart, Prince! With Ludmila you
Must hasten on the homeward road;
Summon new strength and fortitude,
And stay to love and honour true.
A heavenly bolt will shatter malice
And put to bed all your distress;
In bright Kiev you will find peace;
The princess, in Vladimir's palace,
From her charmed sleep will find release.'

*

Enlivened, Ruslan gently lifted
His wife, then carried down the path
This love he'd lost, now newly gifted;
Mounted his steed; behind them drifted
The place of doleful living death.

So, bearing in his arms this precious
Burden, the sleeping girl as fresh as
The dawn, the dwarf trussed at
    the back,
They took the silent homeward track.
A breeze traversing the deserted
Barrens ruffled her hair in play,
With the gold ringlets gently flirted;
How often could he hear her sighing!
How often secret lovedreams chose
To show in her pale features, dyeing
Her cheeks with momentary rose!
He, in enchanted contemplation,
From gazing at her never swerved,
Smiles, tears, and above all observed
Her soft, lush bosom's agitation . . .

*

Meanwhile, through dale and over hill,
In the bright day and the night's chill,
Our hero wends his way, unceasing.
The distance homewards seems increasing,
And the girl sleeps. Did Ruslan, young,
Burning in his suppressed desire,
Who'd suffered so much for so long,
Remain content with taking care
Of her, or when the flame burnt strong
Resist no more, but come to glory?
He did, the monk says, who consigned to
The written word our hero's story
– Resist, that is! And I'm inclined to
Believe him! For a coarse and sorry
Affair is lust assuaged alone,
We need to share in love's caresses;
Ludmila's kind of sleep was one
Unlike yours, nymphs and shepherdesses,
In woodland shadows languishing
And warmed by the sweet fires of spring.
A glade's still green in memory's keeping,
Birches around, a summer night,
And Lida, who was my delight,

Slept or pretended to be sleeping . . .
Ah, that first kiss of youthful passion,
Tremulous, over-hasty, light –
Was it too soon, too late, too slight?
My friends, she slept on, in her fashion! . . .
I babble nonsense; it's enough!
What point recalling love long over,
All of its joys, all of its grief?
Give me a moment to recover . . .
Now others, more immediate, press:
Chernomor, Ruslan, the princess.

They rode across a valley, starkly
Devoid of life but for a few
Wide-scattered firs. Beyond it, darkly
Outlined against the sky's clear blue,
A gloomy mound; and Ruslan knew
At once he was again approaching
The head. His steed more restive grew
But speeded up, its great hooves scorching
The level ground. Soon Ruslan gazed
Close up, and saw its eyes were glazed;
Its hair was like a grim, black forest
That grew out of, or rather clung

To soil, of all on earth the poorest –
Its brow and cheeks, all colour wrung
From them bar the dark grey of lead.
Its monstrous lips were widely parted,
Showing clenched teeth. It clung to life,
Though death's grim business had started.
Ruslan rides close, with dwarf and wife,
And cries: 'Good morning, head! I'm here!
May I present my prisoner?
I'm glad you've got the chance to see and
Know he is punished, the foul fiend
Who so betrayed you!' As the prince's
Proud words to him sink in, the head,
Stony and feelingless, evinces
Signs of new life, awakening
It seems; the glazed eyes can now see,
They know this warrior and that thing,
Its brother; moans in agony.
Its nostrils flare, a sudden blaze
Of crimson surges to the wax
Cheeks, and its swiftly dying gaze
A final anguished fury racks.
In torment, in deep agitation,
It grinds its teeth, then struggles to
Offer, although no sound comes through,

To the trussed dwarf an imprecation.
But this, now, is its final hour;
The flame of life goes out in seconds
And its long suffering ends here,
As first its heavy breathing weakens;
Then the small change, but so profound,
In the grim face; a shuddering sound,
Then to eternal sleep and peace ...
Ruslan is silent as that place
Of dolour slips away behind them;
Shuddering, the dwarf scarce dares to breathe,
But prays that his familiars find him,
And when they do ... His black thoughts seethe.

In the cool darkness of a wood
Above a nameless river stood
A peasant hut, neglected, faded,
By a dense clump of pine trees shaded.
The stream was sluggish, nothing stirred,
No sound but for its gentle frottage
Against a reed fence, feeble guard
Made to protect the peasant cottage.
Even the slight breeze had been schooled
To hush; dark, lost in isolation,

This covert, since the world's creation,
You'd guess, by silence had been ruled.
Ruslan drew up and made encampment,
For all was quiet and serene;
The rising sun brought an enchantment
Of wider views, the shoreline green,
Shimmering through light morning mist,
And sparkling waters fed contentment.
He laid his wife on the smooth grass
And sat beside, as at a tryst
Of lovers, sighed with tenderness
And longing. Suddenly a boat's
Small sail appears, and to him floats
The singing of a fisherman;
He watches him; he's cast his seine,
Now bends to ply his oars and gain
The shore; he beaches, and Ruslan
Sees running from the hut a slender
Young woman, her hair unconfined,
Flowing as nature has designed,
Breasts bare, her eyes and smile tender –
You know by instinct she is kind,
Everything's sweet and good about her.
She and the fisherman embrace,
And lie together by the water,

Body to body, face to face;
An hour then of unhurried leisure
They spend, enjoying love and pleasure.
But who's the happy fisherman
The mute, astonished Prince Ruslan
Slowly begins to recognise?
It is Ratmir, the Khazar Khan,
Who has abandoned thirst for glory;
Ratmir, his rival for the prize
Of the princess, prepared for gory
Battle erstwhile with him; Ratmir,
Who in this tranquil, lonely spot
Fame and Ludmila has forgot,
Choosing the love he has found here.

Ruslan approached, and Ratmir gazed,
Stood up, half-recognised that face,
Then with a joyous shout, amazed,
Rushed to his friend and they embrace.
'What do I see?' Ruslan asks, teasing.
'Your sword, that always gained fresh lustre,
Always the first when armies muster:
Gone now! Is solitude more pleasing?'
'My friend,' replies the fisherman,

'I grew bored with the clash of steel,
I came to realise, Ruslan,
That fame in battle is unreal.
Believe me, an innocent occupation,
Love, in this woodland isolation,
Are dearer to me a hundredfold.
My bloodlust was a rabid bitch;
Bitten by it no more, I'm rich,
Rich in the happiness I hold.
I have forgotten all, dear friend,
Even Ludmila, in the end!'
'Dear Khan,' said Ruslan, 'I'm astonished –
But glad for you; she's with me here.'
'Ludmila! . . . How . . .?' His colour
        vanished.

'The princess! With you here! But where?
I'd love to see her – no, that's madness;
This lovely girl . . . she's very dear
To me; she cured my wretched sadness,
She is my life, she is my joy,
She's brought me back the innocence
I last had when I was a boy,
And love – love that alone makes sense
Of the mad world. She saved me from
The coils of twelve enchanting girls,

In love with me, their kisses warm,
Their forms voluptuous, their teeth pearls,
Their eyes . . . But there was too much pleasure,
Too much . . . I left them all for her,
For they were amorous beyond all measure,
And I much like a prisoner.
Forgetting fame and enemies,
I love this silence and these trees,
The depths almost impenetrable;
I'm peaceful here, my name unknown,
Living with you, my love, my own,
Only with you, light of my soul!'

The peasant girl, a shepherdess,
With them throughout, and keenly listening,
Gazed always at her lover's face,
Smiling and sighing, her eyes glistening.

The knight and fisherman, till nightfall,
Sat by the river, running through
Old times, the sad days, the delightful,
In heartfelt union; the hours flew.
The woods that stretch above them darken;

In moonlight, all is silent, still,
However keenly one might hearken.
High time to go: against the chill
A cover's laid on the princess
Asleep, then Ruslan mounts. The Khan,
In spirit rides out at his side
In thoughtful mood, sends to Ruslan
His wish that he find happiness,
Love, fame, and triumphs far and wide . . .
He's happy with the path he's taken,
But wistful thoughts of youth and pride
Involuntarily awaken.

During the friends' long reminiscence
A figure rose who brought a laugh
From both of them – craven Farlaf.
Skulking at home, beating his peasants,
He still, recovering from fear,
Wanted Ludmila ardently,
And prayed Naïna would appear.
She came, and croaked, 'Remember me?
Saddle your horse; I'll lead, you follow.
I'll help you get the girl.' With that,
The old witch changed into a cat

And raced off over ditch and hollow,
Turning at times her eyes, sly, bright,
To guide Farlaf's horse through the night.

Ruslan passed through a dreaming valley,
The silence of the night profound,
Between the clouds the moon would rally
And shed light on a burial mound.
As often, sadness gripped his heart
As he looked down upon the sleeper
So close, yet sleep kept them apart;
His gloomy thoughts grew ever deeper,
Sliding to dreaminess until
Sleep mingled, imperceptible;
Its cool wings threatened to encumber
Him as he gazed with drooping eyes
Down at his wife; he tried to raise
His head, but then was lost in slumber.

He dreams a dream that's like a spasm
That jerks the heart and makes it fail:
Ludmila stands above a chasm,
No movement from her, her face pale . . .

And suddenly she's disappeared,
Above the chasm he alone;
And then her piteous cry is heard,
Calling on him from fathoms down …
Ruslan descends to save his wife,
Down, down, into the fearful murkiness …
Makes ground … and thanks to dreaming's
    quirkiness
There is Vladimir to the life,
And it's his palace, high, a-sparkle,
It's feast-time, and he's in a circle
Of twelve young sons and noted guests,
But there's no talk, no roars, no jests,
The old prince seems as bleak, or bleaker
Than on the day that broke his heart;
None dares to quaff mead from his beaker,
Nor cough, nor reach for pie or tart.
Ruslan now notices Rogdai
Among the silent guests, long after
He'd sent him, lifeless, down to lie
In water. Alone he, goblet frothing,
Drinks deep from it, too drunk to see
Ruslan, the object of his loathing.
Even Ratmir is seen to be
In this strange crowd, and other friends

And foes. And now the lyric
Strains of Bayan are heard as he
Sings of old times and deeds heroic.
Amidst the rippling minstrelsy
Into the feast-hall strides Farlaf,
Leading Ludmila by the hand;
And yet her father does not stand
Or give the least impression of
Joy at her being saved, his head
Is sunken still, deeply despairing,
A gloom that all around are sharing,
Keeping the silence of the dead.
All vanishes . . . A mortal cold
Is stalking through our sleeping hero;
The heavy dream's so taken hold
That down his cheeks run tears of sorrow.
He tells himself: a dream, no more!
Can't wake! As one by strong tides pulled
Swims towards a receding shore.

The moon is dim above the hill,
The forest dark as Ruslan's mood is,
The vale beneath is deathly still . . .
And riding through it is his Judas.

*

A glade before him shows up, hazy,
And then some sort of hump or mound;
Riderless horse . . . at closer gaze he
Sees – heavens! – Ludmila on the
       ground,
Asleep, it seems; Ruslan too, fast
Asleep, and at her feet. The coward
Is fearful, for in the mist he's lost
Sight of the witch-cat; inches forward,
Dropping the reins, clasping his sword
In his cold, shaking hand, prepared
To cleave the knight. No battle – *finis*!
Ruslan's horse, sensing danger, whinnies
And paws the ground. But nothing can
Arouse from his deep sleep Ruslan,
It weighs on him with cruel persistence;
Leaning above, the villain stabs
The prince three times between the ribs,
Then swiftly rides into the distance,
Frightened in case his victim rise,
But bearing off the precious prize.

*

Ruslan lay all night, feeling nothing,
As mist entombed the burial mound.
Blood flowed, creating streamlets, frothing,
From every suppurating wound.
At dawn he saw but, his brain stunned,
Knew only there was something strange here,
And let out a weak, heavy groan;
Struggled to get up, face the danger,
But fell back, breath and motion done.

CANTO SIX

My tender girl, my heart's desire,
You crave again my carefree lyre,
Bid me to sing of olden times,
To spend the hours of priceless leisure
On teasing from my Muse new
        rhymes.
But you should know, my only
        treasure,
I care no more to be confined
To lonely toil, perfecting style,
Bent to a page, when all the while
I'm drunk on you! I have resigned
From everything except the passion

We know together: I breathe *you*!
Away with fame, that fool of fashion;
The lofty phrases disinherit
Your humble friend; genius withdrew,
Such as it was, that airy spirit,
When you appeared; I'm deaf and blind
To all but you: you flood my mind.
And yet you wish – no, you implore,
Loving my tales beyond belief –
More of Ruslan and Chernomor,
Vladimir, and the Finn's long grief,
Ludmila, the old witch, and so on;
You say they charm you, even glow on
Your eyelids when you sleep and dream;
I believe that; at times you seem,
When listening to my crazy stuff,
Though smiling, clearly nodding off.
Yet other times my lazy voice
A tenderer expression brings,
And so, besotted, I've no choice:
I'll pluck again the stubborn strings;
I'll sit down at your tiny feet;
With them young Ruslan will compete.

*

But wait! I left Ruslan dead. Heavens!
Stone-dead upon the mournful field;
The blood that poured out has congealed,
Above his body circle ravens;
Silent his horn, still are his sword
And helmet with its flourished beard.

His steed walks round and round
     its master
Quite lost: there's no one to explain;
Its eyes have lost their fiery lustre,
Lowered, the proud head's golden mane;
It does not frisk, it does not bound,
But simply waits for him to rise,
But Ruslan's sleep is too profound,
His shield reflects the sombre skies.

There's someone else alive of course:
Chernomor in the saddle-bag,
Unseen, forgotten by the hag
Naïna, and just like the horse
Ignorant of all. He, bored and weary,
Afraid out loud to vent his fury

At Ruslan, curses silently.
At long last he decides to see
What's going on – peeps out – O wonder!
He sees the knight is lying dead,
Soaked in his own congealed blood;
Ludmila's vanished, someone's plunder;
The old dwarf shudders joyously
And laughs, and croaks, 'I'm free, I'm free!'
So sure about what lies ahead!

Meanwhile, with mix of hope and terror,
Grateful to have the witch's aid,
Rides Farlaf, Kiev ever nearer;
The girl across his saddle laid,
The enchanted and enchanting sleeper,
Hears not the roaring, restless Dnieper;
He can see Kiev's golden domes
And soon he's there: the city hums,
A crowd around them closely pressing;
The news is borne along before,
And shouts resound, their joy expressing;
Now he is at the palace door.

*

Vladimir Bright-Sun at that hour,
Burdened by his unchanging grief,
Was seated in his lofty tower,
Accompanied by all his chief
Counsellors, boyars grave and pompous,
When suddenly they heard a rumpus
Down in the courtyard: acclamation,
Shrieks, shouts of joyful celebration.
The door flew open and a squire
Unknown to them burst in; unused
To interruptions they're confused –
Murmurs exchanged, these rising higher,
Hearing what's happened; they're bemused,
Ludmila found – untold delight,
'But by Farlaf! Can this be right?'
Vladimir, who's been mutely listening,
Looks younger by a score of years,
Although his eyes with tears are glistening;
He hastens to go down the stairs
To his dear daughter, his breath rasping
From forcing his old legs to move
Swiftly; his only thought is love,
That in a moment he'll be clasping
Her to him. But he finds Ludmila,
Unaware that he leans above,

Gently supported by a killer
Who holds a finger to his lips;
'Be careful,' Farlaf says, 'she sleeps.
The brute who stole her thought the surest
Hideout would be a Murom forest:
A wicked goblin. I discovered
Them there, good Prince. The full moon rose
On three nights as the battle hovered,
But wickedness was bound to lose.
I found her thus; she's not recovered;
Who might help cure this strange dormition,
Or when she will awake, who knows?
Fate knows the answers, I suppose.
Hope, patience, prayers for her condition:
No comforts do we have but those.'

The fateful news begins to ripple
Throughout the town from tongue to tongue,
And swiftly half of Kiev's people
The square before the palace throng;
Its splendid doors are opened wide,
All jostle, push, to crowd inside
To see their poor princess, displayed
On a high couch of rich brocade;

Her sleep, it seems, could not be deeper
This side of death; around the sleeper
Are knights and princes wearing holy
Expressions, their heads lowered; horn,
Dulcimer, drum and tambourine
Play over her a melancholy
Tribute; the old prince, weak from grief,
His grey head resting at her feet,
Weeps silently. Nearby, Farlaf
Is also looking desolate,
And trembles, fearing every shadow;
Is touched by guilt, distress, regret,
Vanished, his brashness, his bravado.

Night fell; but no one in the city
Was in the mood for sleep; they pressed
Closely together and discussed
Her plight with wonderment and pity;
Neighbour with neighbour, brother with brother,
Met at street corners, talked together,
Leaving young wives to chat alone.
And when the two-horned moon grew dimmer
Then vanished in the light of dawn
A new alarm began to simmer,

Shouts rang out, house to house, and all
Rushed pell-mell to the city wall,
And there they saw, through morning mist,
White tents beyond the river flutter,
Horsemen appear from every quarter,
Shields flashing sunlight, and black dust
Kicked up by carts and all the clutter
Of an invading host; camp fires
Flame on the hilltops, and suggest
To fearful Kiev its own pyres!

But that same hour, with a calm heart,
The master of all magic art
Sat in his cave devoid of sun,
Knowing the day by fate elected
And by the Finnish seer predicted
Had unavoidably begun.

Deep in the sun-parched steppe, encompassed
By a long chain of barren hills,
The realm of windstorm, raging tempest,
A landscape where foreboding fills
Even witches in late wanderings,

There lies a wondrous, hidden vale,
And in the vale there are two springs:
In one the waters never stale,
It gurgles over stones and sings;
The other spring holds stagnant water;
Never the wind blows, not a breath,
No vernal coolness can be sought here,
The ancient pines stand still as death;
No birds sing, and no fawn dares tread
The water's edge to quench its thirst.
Two spirits have stood here since first
The world began, guarding the dead
And living springs in silence, charmed.
A grizzled traveller stands there, armed
With an empty pitcher in each hand;
He breaks the spell, the guards awaken
From their long sleep, don't understand
And run off quickly, deeply shaken.
He fills the vessels from the pure
And the stale springs, then rises, flying
From this vale to another, far,
And in two seconds he's before
Prince Ruslan in his own blood lying.
He stoops and, on each gaping wound,
The old man sprinkles the dead water,

Which seals it, clears all putrid matter,
And rosy skin blooms all around;
When living water starts to play
On the corpse then, cheerful, healthy,
    spritely,
Ruslan stands up, in all his knightly
Vigour and youth, to a new day,
Looking around him, his eyes eager,
And sleep's dark shades which might
    disfigure
This bright day's life just melt away.
But where's Ludmila? He's alone!
His heart quails, all his strength is gone;
But the next moment his heart races:
The Finn is with him and embraces
Him with, 'What fate willed has come true,
My son! You can expect great blessing;
A bloody feast is summoning you;
Your potent sword will be redressing
Much wrong; on Kiev gentle peace
Will fall; Ludmila is there now;
This ring I give you: touch her brow
With it and she will find release
From the dark power of the effusion
Which holds her bound in sleep. Just seeing

Your face appear will sow confusion
Among your foes and send them fleeing.
Good will prevail, evil take flight;
May you both merit happiness.
And so farewell – a long one, knight!
Give me your hand ... When we
    both pass
The grave – then we shall meet again.'
With that he vanished. Beyond measure
Thrilled and delighted, Ruslan lifted
His arm to thank him for the treasure
Of life, but only silence drifted
Across the field he held alone
Save for his steed, which to him ran
Whinnying, and doubtless frightening
The dwarf still in the bag. Ruslan
Was mounted straight, and on the wing,
Feeling the grass beneath them spring,
Feeling that life had just begun.

But what is happening in Kiev?
Most of the city's folk remain
Clustered on walls and towers to see if
The Pechenegs that fill the plain

Have moved, and dread the Prince of
    heaven,
Wrathful at sinning, has been driven
To punish them with devastation;
In lanes, fear breathes from every stone;
In houses, quiet lamentation;
Alone the father keeps, with sorrow,
The vigil none but he must keep;
His knights make ready for the morrow,
When many more than she will sleep.

And with the dawn the host came surging
Down from the hills, across the plain,
The rear ranks those before them urging
In a tumultuous rush to gain
Superiority at once
Through boldness and relentless force
And reach the ramparts. Straight to horse,
As trumpets break the city's trance,
Its soldiery piles out, confronts
The Turkic host; they clash in battle,
At smell of death the horses rear,
Sword against armour, metal on metal,
And arrows whistle through the air;

Fighters who started in close order
Turn into isolated groups;
Rivers of blood make footing harder,
And here and there a horseman stoops
To kill a knight who's been unseated;
Riderless horses, terrified,
Charge through the field from side to side;
A Russian falls, a Pecheneg,
Here lies a head, and there a leg;
Here someone poleaxed by a mace,
An arrow's split this fellow's face;
Another, fallen, lightly gashed,
Beneath a bolting horse is crushed;
War cries resound and screams of anguish.
The fighting lasts till it's so dark
Comrade from foe they can't distinguish,
Only the grisly mounds that mark
The piles of bodies. But it's best
To close one's tired eyes on these;
The warriors crumple to their knees,
Then sprawl, and sleep soon numbs each
      breast;
Rarely is heard the groans, the pleas
To end a pain too hard to bear,
Or softly murmured Russian prayer.

119

*

Darkness turns slowly into pallor,
The day unsure it should be born,
The east is misty and forlorn,
The river has a silvery colour.
The mist clears, and some streaks of blue
Now the dispersing clouds show through.
Woods, hills, appear, a gradual clearance,
But still the foe in sleep are locked,
Calm, confident, to all appearance.
But of a sudden they are shocked
To instant life by loud horn-blowing;
All scramble to reach sword and spear;
Soon, sounds of battle, ever growing,
Confuse the Kievans who peer
From walls and ramparts: it's not clear
What's causing this ferocious drama;
Gaps form with an amazing speed,
Men felled, it seems, by one swift blade;
And then they see a knight in armour
That flames like lightning, on his steed;
He rides and reaps, his bright sword flashing,
Cutting and hewing, thrusting, slashing,
And at the same time blows his horn.

It is Ruslan. God's thunderbolt,
He falls on them, this man reborn,
With the dwarf feeling every jolt
Behind; wherever the sword whistles,
So swift it's neither seen nor felt,
The pagan knights are lopped like thistles;
And in no time the plain is filled
With men his magic sword has killed
Or wounded, or his steed has ground them,
Weapons and armour strewn around them.
From city walls the trumpets' roar
Frees the impatient Slavic forces,
They race to add to Ruslan's score,
With curdling cries, thunder of horses;
The Pechenegs become a rabble;
These wild descendants of long-dead
Invaders, their will shattered, scrabble
To gather horses that have fled –
And now the horde itself is fleeing,
Trampling on their own kin who fell,
Kievan war cries all agreeing
The infidels will burn in hell.
Kiev exults, and cheers the mighty
Swordsman, resplendent warrior;
His lance is glittering like a star,

Blood-trickles add to the strange light he
Seems to be bathed in; and a beard
Flows from his bronze helm – also weird.
'Ruslan! Ruslan!' the townsfolk call as,
With the fresh vigour hope can bring,
Amid the whoops and hollerings
He all but flies towards the palace.
Into the silent room he strides
Where the entranced Ludmila sleeps;
Vladimir still his vigil keeps,
Kneeling in grief; none else besides,
His knights have rushed off to the battle.
There's one knight, though, who guards the door;
Childish, he thinks, to test one's mettle
In the alarms and shocks of war:
Farlaf was needed here much more.
Seeing Ruslan his face turns ashen,
Opens his mouth but nothing's heard,
Falls to his knees, awaits the sword:
Death in his own cold-blooded fashion . . .
But Ruslan wastes no glance, no word,
But rushes on to his Ludmila,
Touches her peaceful, slumbering
Brow tremulously with the ring,
The secret ring . . . a prayer to will her

To waken ... and lo, wondrously,
She wakes, she opens her bright eyes!
She stretched and yawned; her sole surprise:
After so long a night's sleep she
Could not recall the vivid dream
That kept her sleeping ... it was dim ...
And then a sudden revelation,
Seeing him there – she'd dreamt of *him*!
They hugged with passion, adoration ...
Ruslan saw nothing, nothing minded,
His soul in rapture; the old Prince
Was both laughing and – it made no sense –
Sobbing; he hugged them, by tears blinded.

How shall I end my lengthy story?
I'm sure you've guessed, my dearest friend!
Since lately it's been somewhat gory
You may be pleased to have an end
Where all is pleasant. His voice quavery,
Farlaf confessed his shameful knavery,
And Ruslan, in his happiness,
Forgave him. Even Chernomor,
His sorcery gone, hence powerless,
Was taken as a courtier;

RUSLAN AND LUDMILA

In palaces, you see, such charmless
Figures abound, servile and harmless,
And he was present when Vladimir
Hosted a feast which lasted ages.

Events described in ancient pages
By some long-perished Russian dreamer.

EPILOGUE

For long now, from the world retreated,
Enjoying blissful, silent days,
With my lyre's help I've celebrated
Deeds of the dark past, tried to raise
The dead to life, and through my verses
Forget the injuries of fate,
The fools, the gossip envy nurses,
The girls I kissed too soon, too late.
I flew away from this our earth
On wings of my imagination
Even as a storm was in gestation
Above my head, and close to birth.
I was quite lost . . . but you preserved me,

Friendship, as you have done since my
First stormy years, tenderly served me
In sickness, sustained my liberty,
The godhead of our fiery youth!
Restored peace always to my heart . . .
From the Nevá, a world apart,
I see before me, proud, uncouth
Mountains, far distant from the art
Of rumour, scandal and untruth,
The mighty Caucasus, their towering
Summits and cataracts of stone,
And in that beauty, gloomy, louring,
I feel afresh and stand alone;
I drink in wild and sullen nature,
And know this wilderness will feature
In my soul's growth, for all is linked –
But poetry's flame is now extinct,
I search in vain for that elation,
It's gone, that quiet, happy time
Of losing self in flowing rhyme;
The time of heartfelt inspiration,
The time of love, its first sweet fever.
The days of rapture are too brief –
And hiding from me now forever
The joyous Muse of love or grief.